I get asked that question more than any other.

"Jeffrey, why is your hair falling out?"
is a close second.

Jeffrey Gitomer's

THE VERY LITTLE BUT VERY POWERFUL BOOK on CLOSING

*Ask the Right Questions, Transfer the Value,
Create the Urgency, and Win the Sale*

WILEY

Cover design: Wiley

Editor: Jennifer Gluckow

This book is printed on acid-free paper. ∞

Published by John Wiley & Sons, Inc., Hoboken, New Jersey.
Published simultaneously in Canada.

Library of Congress Cataloging-in-Publication Data:

Gitomer, Jeffrey H.
   The very little but very powerful book on closing : ask the right questions, transfer the value, create the urgency, and win the sale / Jeffrey Gitomer.
     pages cm
   Includes index.
   ISBN 978-1-118-98652-3 (hardback)
 1. Selling.   I. Title.
   HF5438.25.G5783 2015
   658.85–dc23

                                                    2015029016

Printed in the United States of America

10 9 8 7 6 5 4 3 2 1

Contents

Can't close the sale? Whose fault is it?

Are you blaming the prospect when you can't close? Are you telling the boss it's the prospect's fault that you can't set an appointment or they won't order now?

After 25 years of selling, training, and consulting, one truth remains – I have yet to hear one salesperson say, "The prospect wouldn't buy and it was my fault" or "The prospect wouldn't appoint me and it was my fault."

You say, "But Jeffrey, you don't understand, my situation is different." Bullshit. The only thing different about your situation is, you'd rather blame someone else than yourself.

If your prospect is constantly telling you …

"Why don't you call back in two weeks?"

"We haven't had a chance to discuss it, call back in three days?"

"Yeah, we're still interested, but it's been real crazy here and …"

"I have to get together with my partner."

"I'm not ready to buy yet."

It ain't their fault, Verne. It's yours.

The key is to accept responsibility for no sale yet and ask questions to get the prospect to tell you more about why he is not deciding. He has not said no, so obviously you have just not answered his questions.

People are worrying about, thinking about, or acting on their stuff. You're worrying about, thinking about, or acting on your stuff. Prospects could care less about your stuff unless they perceive the need or a benefit to themselves. (Selfish, but true.)

When a prospect says, "I'll know by Thursday at 1:00 p.m." it becomes a benchmark time and date for the salesperson – a deadline. When you come to understand that the date and time commitment mean virtually nothing to the prospect, you're on your way to accepting responsibility as a salesperson.

When you follow up the next time, take a proactive stance to hold them to what they said. If they're going to decide by Tuesday, ask "Could I drop by Wednesday at 10:00 a.m. to get the good news in person?"

At some point, after you have been through the close several times with the prospect, you have to realize that you have very little to lose. You may have to be real direct and ask them if they are going to buy or not. You can't keep wining and dining them for the next year. It's not worth the time or effort.

Well, what if they are just the kind of person that hates to say no? Be up front with them, but be understanding as well. You still need to ask the questions to find out why they are postponing the decision.

You must be willing to take a risk to get to the true objection. If you don't think the sale will be made anyway, take more risk. Use tough sales or no sales as learning experiences. See how far you can go to get the truth.

When the sale is over and you have lost, be willing to accept the responsibility for the process, hold your head high, and move on to help the next prospect.

The real truths hurt ... are you ready for all six of them?

1. You haven't created enough need.

2. You haven't uncovered the real objection.

3. You haven't created enough urgency.

4. You haven't convinced him of the benefits of ownership.

5. You haven't built enough trust.

6. You haven't built enough confidence ... have you?

What to do? (and not do)

- Don't blame it on the prospect.
- Don't moan about what the prospect's excuse is.
- Figure out what the true objection is.
- Figure out a solution for that objection.
- Try your best to overcome that objection to make the sale this time.
- AND be sure you prevent that objection from recurring the next time.

The burden is on you. If you want to sell professionally, get real about who is at fault when a sale isn't made. Get a mirror. Get responsible.

People are worrying about, thinking about, or acting on their stuff. You're worrying about, thinking about, or acting on your stuff. Prospects could care less about your stuff unless they perceive the need or a benefit to themselves. (Selfish but true.)

Jeffrey Gitomer

How to ask a closing question.

Thousands of pages have been written on closing the sale. You can have the best presentation in the world, you can be an expert in your product or your field of endeavor, but if you don't know how to close the sale, dining out for you will probably mean a drive-thru window.

The experts (J. Douglas Edwards, Zig Ziglar, Earl Nightingale, etc.) define closing as: Asking a question, the answer to which confirms the sale. After you ask this all important question, it is critical you follow the golden rule of selling …

After you ask a closing question, SHUT-UP! The next person who speaks, loses.

Jeffrey Gitomer

There are thousands of ways to ask for the sale. (We'll cover many of the classic closes in future articles.) An important guideline in asking for the sale is to try to eliminate "no" as a possible response to your question. You may not get the coveted "yes" as a result of eliminating the word "no," but you will get dialog or objections that will eventually lead to a yes.

Formulate your closing question in a way that responds to the prospect's main need or desire. For example … Mr. Jones, "Would you like these t-shirts in light or dark colors?" Or, "Would you like delivery before or after the first of next month?" Or, "Did you want the model with automatic remote control or manual control?" These three examples are using the *alternative of choice method*. A simple technique that eliminates "no" as a response.

Other closing questions offer a possible "no" response. Before you ask this type of closing question, be sure you have confirmed the prospect's interest, and he has given you concrete buying signals. For example … You're selling Mr. Jones a fax machine. Jones says he needs a machine by Tuesday, but has not said he was buying from you. Salesman asks, "Would you like me to deliver your new fax machine Monday evening?" That is a solid closing question. You have given the prospect the option of saying no, but it is unlikely he'll use it. (Even if Jones says "no," then ask "When would be the most convenient time to make delivery?")

The key is to ask for the sale in a sincere, friendly manner. Don't push or use high pressure. If you just stop talking after you ask the closing question, the tension in the air mounts real fast. A minute seems like an hour when the room is silent.

Jeffrey Gitomer

Self-confidence is important. The buyer will buy if you believe he will. Most salespeople don't ask for the sale because they're afraid of rejection, uncomfortable about the money, or aren't sharp enough to recognize the buying signals of a customer.

In my experience, I have found the biggest flaw in failing to secure the order is the salesperson's inability to know when to ask for it. The rule of thumb is … ask early and ask often.

Can you close a sale in five questions?

Questions breed sales. Using questions to find facts is critical to creating an atmosphere in which a sale can be made. Sales solutions are easy once you identify the prospect's problems. The sale is most easily made once you identify the prospect's real needs.

Here is a questioning technique that can be used to qualify, identify true needs, and close the sale in five question-steps. For this example, let's say I'm selling printing.

(Have a note pad out and use it as the prospect responds.)

Question one: "Mr. prospect, how do you select a printer" (variation "how do you choose a printer")?

Prospect says, "Quality, delivery, and price."

Question two: "How do you define quality?" Or, "What does quality mean to you?" (Ask the same *how do you define* question for all three responses of the *how do you choose* question.)

The prospect will give you thoughtful answers. Many prospects have never been asked questions like these, and will be forced to think in new patterns. You may even want to ask a follow–up question or create a tie–down question here before going to question three. For example, the prospect says he defines quality as crisp, clear printing. You ask, "Oh, you mean printing that reflects the image of the quality of your company?"

How can a prospect possibly say no to that question?

Question three: "Is that important to you?" Or, "Is that most important to you?" Or, "Why is that important to you?"

This question draws out the true need of the prospect. Finding out what is important to them about printing, and why printing is important, are the keys to closing the sale. There may be secondary or follow–up questions to gain clear definition of what is important and why.

Question four: "If I could deliver the quality you demand, so that the image in your printing reflects the image of your business to your customers, and I could do it in the time frame you require, at a reasonable (not the cheapest) price, would I be (variation: is there any reason I would not be) a candidate for your business?"

Of course you would! This is a feedback question that combines the data found in the first three questions. It's the classic "If I … would you?" question that makes the prospect commit. It actually quasi-closes the prospect. If there is a true objection (we have to get bids, someone else decides, I'm satisfied with my present vendor), it is likely to surface here.

Question five: "Great! When could we begin?" Or, "Great! When is your next printing project?"

The object of the fifth question is to pin the prospect down to a beginning date or time or quantity to start doing business. In many cases you can sell a sample order or trial. Where big ticket products are involved (copiers, computers), a puppy dog approach will work best (leave your product for the customer to use for a few days), or take the prospect to visit a satisfied customer and see your product in operation and get a live testimonial.

This is not hard sell, it's heart sell. Good questions get to the heart of the problem/ need very quickly without the buyer feeling like he or she is being pushed.

Jeffrey Gitomer

Use the questioning process early and often.

Jeffrey Gitomer

If you're doing a lot of talking and the prospect is not – you're boring the prospect and losing the sale.

Jeffrey Gitomer

Looking for a few additional power question lead-ins?

Try these:

- What do you look for …
- What have you found …
- How do you propose …
- What has been your experience …
- How have you successfully used …
- How do you determine …
- Why is that a deciding factor …
- What makes you choose …
- What do you like about …
- What is one thing you would improve about …
- What would you change about … (Do not say, "What don't you like about …")
- Are there other factors …
- What does your competitor do about …
- How do your customers react to …

To use questions successfully, they must be thought out and written down in advance. Develop a list of 15–25 questions that uncover needs, problems, pains, concerns, and objections. Develop 15–25 more that create prospect commitment as a result of the information you have uncovered.

Practice. After about 25 attempts at asking the right questions, you'll begin to see the real rewards.

Want to close more sales? Listen more!

How many of you ever had a course in listening skills? How-to-listen lessons were never offered as part of any formal education. It's amazing … the skills we need the most are never taught in school.

We listen to TV, radio, and CDs, and we can recite chapter and verse the next day, or sing the songs word for word. But if your spouse or child says something, you say, "What?" or "I didn't hear you."

How often do you ask someone to repeat what they said? How often do you hear, "You weren't listening to a word I said."

The two biggest impediments to listening are:

1. I often have an opinion (of you or what you're going to say) before I begin listening.
2. I often have made up my mind before I begin listening, or before I hear the full story.

The two important rules of effective listening must be observed in this order or you will not be an effective listener.

1. Listen with the intent to understand.

Then

2. Listen with the intent to respond.

Think about the way you listen.

- Are you listening with one ear or two? (Half-listening means doing something while someone else is talking.)
- Are you doing something else when someone is speaking?
- Do you have your mind on something else when someone is speaking?
- Do you fake listening so you can get in your comments?
- Are you waiting for a pause to get in your response?

At some point you stop listening. When does that occur?

- After you have formulated your response.
- After you have been turned off by the speaker.
- When you decide to interrupt someone to say something.
- When the person speaking isn't saying anything you want to hear.

Here are 14 guidelines to observe that will maximize your listening skills, increase your productivity, reduce errors, gain customer satisfaction, and help you make more sales.

1. Don't interrupt. (But … but … but.)

2. Ask questions. Then be quiet. Concentrate on really listening.

3. Prejudice will distort what you hear. Listen without prejudging.

4. Use eye contact and listening noises ("mmhmm," "hmm," "gee," "I see," "oh") to show the other person you're listening.

5. Don't jump to the answer before you hear the ENTIRE situation.

6. Listen for purpose, details, and conclusions.

7. Active listening involves interpreting. Interpret quietly.

8. Listen to what is not said. Implied is often more important than spoken.

9. Think between sentences.

10. Digest what is said (and not said) before engaging your mouth.

11. Ask questions to be sure you understood what was said or meant.

12. Ask questions to be sure the speaker said all he/she wanted to say.

13. Demonstrate you are listening by taking action.

14. If you're thinking during speaking, think solution. Don't embellish the problem.

What causes people not to listen?

- Sometimes people are afraid to hear what is about to be said, so they block it out. Don't be afraid to listen.

- Sometimes you take the other person for granted – spouse, parent, child.

- Sometimes you're mentally preoccupied with other things.

- Sometimes you're just rude.

- Sometimes the person grates on you, so you don't listen.

- Sometimes you have other things on your mind.

- Sometimes you know the person speaking, and have prejudged them.

- Sometimes you don't respect the other person and block the listening process.

- Sometimes you think you already know what is about to be said.

- Sometimes you think you know it all … or is that all the time?

> There are many secrets to becoming a good listener, but the one that simplifies them all is: Just shut-up!
>
> *Jeffrey Gitomer*

IMPORTANT NOTE

Assuming the sale is a state of mind, it does not preclude employing the science of selling. Yes, you must, from time to time, use sales techniques, but it's more a matter of word choice and delivery than trying to master some close that has a name.

"The Benjamin Franklin Close," "The Sharp Angle Close," and "The Final Question Close" are all old-world methods of selling. These tactics will make people mad, or uncomfortable, or both. You may even occasionally make a sale – but no one will ever refer their friends to go through the same ordeal.

MORE IMPORTANT NOTE

The close of a sale is only one step in the sales cycle. You don't just close a sale – you lead up to a close. You earn the sale based on what you have said and done to guide the prospect to a decision.

MOST IMPORTANT NOTE

The actual close of a sale is a delicate balance between your words and actions, and the prospect's thoughts and perceptions.

A sale is always made – either you sell them on yes – or they sell you on no.

Jeffrey Gitomer

You can't get the sale 'til you ask for it.

Seems too simple. Just ask.

In most cases to get the sale – at some point you must ask for it. "Yes, Jeffrey," you say, "but when do you ask? What's the perfect time to ask?"

How do I know? No one knows that except you. I can only tell you it's a delicate combination of the prospect's buying signals, and your gut feeling.

How and what to ask are easier to define than when. Since the "ask" is a critical part of the sale, you'd better be prepared with a number of options for the how and what parts.

IMPORTANT NOTE

Here's what never to ask – "What will it take for me to get your business?" or "What will it take to earn your business?" That's an insult question. Great salespeople figure out what it takes, and then do it.

MORE IMPORTANT NOTE

Many salespeople are "ask-reluctant." If this is you, just realize the worst that can happen when you ask is that the prospect says, "No" – which to any good salesperson means "Not yet!" Big deal.

MOST IMPORTANT NOTE

Ask for the sale when the mood is right. The worst possible place is in the prospect's office. Best place is a business breakfast, lunch, or dinner. Next best is your office. Next best is a trade show.

How do you ask for the sale? Here are 7.5 ways ...

1. Ask – What's the risk? When you ask the prospect what risks are associated in doing business with you, real objections surface – or – (and here's the best part), there are usually none that come to mind. You say – "Well, Mr. Johnson, when would you like to start not risking?" and the sale is yours.

2. Ask – When is the next job? If you're making a sale where there are lots of opportunities (printer, supplies, temp help, construction, graphic design), you only need to get one job (order) to prove yourself.

3. Ask for an indirect commitment – Could you arrange your schedule to be there at delivery? How many people will need to be trained? When can we set up training? (This is the assumptive position, explained in-depth in an earlier chapter.)

4. Ask – What's preventing it? Is there anything preventing you from doing business with us? What's in the way? What are the obstacles?

5. If there's an obstacle or objection ask – Is that the only reason? In other words, Mr. Johnson, if it wasn't for [objection], then we could ...

6. Ask or communicate creatively – Go to the 5¢ & 10¢ store (pretty much dates me, doesn't it?) and buy some plastic fence and a few plastic (rubber) people. Wire one person to the fence that most resembles (or would be non-offensive to) the prospect. Send it in a box to the prospect – and include a flyer declaring it's "National Get Off the Fence Week." Tell the prospect he's been thinking about it long enough – and what better time to get off the fence, and place an order than during this special celebration week? Tell him he'll be helping underprivileged salespeople all over the world by getting off the fence and placing an order.

Create some laughter.
Have some fun.
Make some sales.

7. Create an offer so good that you can end by asking, "Fair enough?" "Mr. Johnson, I don't know if we can help you or not, but bring your most important examples to lunch on Friday, and if I can help you, I'll tell you. And if I can't help you, I'll tell you that, too. Fair enough?" Here's another – "Mr. Johnson, give me a trial order and let me earn your business. If it's not everything I claim and more, you don't have to pay for it. Fair enough?" ("Fair enough" should always be accompanied by a "can't say no deal.")

And when all else fails:

7.5 Ask with humor – "Mr. Johnson, I finally figured out what it will take to get your business – all you have to do is say yes!" The more adventurous salesperson will add – "When would you like to do that?"

The rule of thumb is: Ask early, and ask often. The best way to master the skill is – practice in front of someone who can say "yes."

Jeffrey Gitomer

What would Ben Franklin think of the Ben Franklin close?

The Benjamin Franklin Close (also known as "The Balance Sheet Close") is one of the classic old-time sales tactics used to close a sale. Never heard of it? Shame on you – not enough sales training.

The scenario is this: You've made your presentation, but the prospect is on the fence, and won't make up his or her mind. You've tried everything, but can't get them to budge.

Then you say, "You know Benjamin Franklin was one of our wisest citizens, wouldn't you agree, Mr. Johnson?" (Get prospect's agreement.) "Whenever he was faced with a decision – and he had some pretty big ones back then – he would take a plain piece of paper, draw a line down the middle, and put a plus (+) on one half, and a minus (–) on the other."

"In his genius, he discovered that by listing all the positive elements on the plus side of the paper, and the negative things on the minus side, the decision would become obvious – pretty sound concept, agreed?" (Get prospect's agreement.)

"Let me show you how it works. Since you're having a tough time deciding, let's list the benefits – some of the reasons you may want to purchase. Then we'll list the negatives. Fair enough?" (Get prospect's agreement.)

Now you list every good thing about your product or service. Get the prospect to say most of them. What the prospect says will be the main points of interest to him. Take your time to develop a complete list. THEN YOU SAY – OK, let's list the negatives, and hand the pen to the prospect and push the list toward him. Don't say a word. Usually the prospect can only think of responses having to do with price or affordability.

In theory, this sounds like a good way to close a sale.

The big problem with the Benjamin Franklin Close – it's old-world selling that not only doesn't work, it annoys the buyer. Try that close on someone who has ever taken a sales course, and it's an insult.

The reality of the sale is – the prospect has already made up his mind – he's just not telling you.

Jeffrey Gitomer

So should you just forget it and never use the Ben Franklin Close? Heck no – just use the Ben Franklin principle in a different way. Do what Ben would have done – figure out a new way and a better way, and use it.

Here's a powerful new way to re-use this classic close. Use it on yourself – before you make the sales call. Use it as a preparation tool. Use it as a strategizing device. Use it to get ready to make a big sale. Get a plain piece of paper (or your laptop), and draw a line down the middle of the page.

On the plus side …

- **List the prospect's main needs.**
- **List the questions you want to ask.**
- **List the benefits and main points you want to be sure to cover.**
- **List one or two personal things in common to discuss.**
- **List the decision makers.**
- **List why you believe they will buy.**

On the minus side …

- **List the reasons why the prospect may not buy – and your responses.**
- **List the obstacles you may have to overcome.**

Now you're ready to make the sale, and Ben helped you.

If you use the Ben Franklin Close on yourself, before you go in to make the sale, then you can ask the buyer intelligent closing questions. For example, questions that might lead with the phrases – What are the major obstacles … or, What would prevent you from …, or, Is there any reason not to proceed with …?

That's a Ben Franklin close that Ben would be proud of – the one you prepare for yourself. You close yourself before you make the sale. Wow!

Try this new version of an old classic. Ben would be proud of you. So would your boss.

I think it was Franklin who said, "A close in time saves nine – objections," but history has distorted it for the people who knit. Pity.

A few closing tactics. Taking a new look at old ways.

Don't close the sale, assume the sale.

The assumptive position is the strongest selling strategy in the world.

By definition, you believe you will make every sale you attempt.

Jeffrey Gitomer

It sounds simple. It is simple – but, it's not easy. In order to utilize the assumptive close, you must be qualified. There are two major prerequisites that make the assumptive close possible:

1. **Your personal preparedness.** You must display self-confidence, have total product knowledge, have a positive mental attitude, exude so much enthusiasm that it's contagious, have a desire to help that exceeds a desire to earn money, and have a genuine sincerity of purpose. If this is 110% you, you're only half way to assumption. Read on …

2. **Your sales preparedness.** There are three strategic areas of sales preparedness, and all must be in place to make assuming the sale possible.

    1. The needs of the prospect have been determined, and are put ahead of yours.

    2. You are established in the mind of the prospect as a person of character, credibility, and high repute. The prospect has confidence in you.

    3. You have built solid rapport with the prospect based on the personal information you've gathered, combined with your knowledge of his business.

Here are six closing strategies and tactics that you might find effective:

1. **Challenge the prospect to do what's best for his business.** This is kind of a guilt strategy. Look the person in the eye and ask him what he thinks is best for his business. This strategy is great when he's doing business with an existing vendor or friend, and they are not providing the best product or service.

2. **We are experts at what we do – and you can have peace of mind to do what you do best, knowing our part of your job will get done.** Tell the prospect that you can help build her business by providing your service and partnering with her. Always let the prospect have a path to doing what they do best, and have peace of mind that your service will supplement that process on their way to success. This strategy is great for selling professional services.

3. **Make a list of objectives for what the prospect wants to accomplish AFTER your product or service is in place.** Your objective as a professional is to get the prospect to see the world as though the sale was already made. Forget about convincing them to do it – that's selling, no one wants to be sold. Show them what their world will be like

after the sale – that's buying, everyone loves to buy. This strategy works on every kind of sale.

4. **Get the prospect to be a visionary.** "Mr. Johnson, if you did, when do you think would be the best time to start?" Let the prospect tell you what he has in mind, instead of you telling him what's on yours. This strategy is called the "if-when decision process," and is great for selling equipment.

5. **Make the prospect commit to a future action.** The traditional method of accomplishing this is: "If I could …, would you …?" but today's professional can't say that exactly – it sounds to salesy. This strategy must be worded more out of conversation than sales presentation. It must be delivered as a desire to help achieve an objective, not a pressure to make a sale.

6. **Make plans for after the sale has taken place, before the sale is consummated.** Even if you don't have the commitment yet, you can try to schedule an installation time, or a meeting after delivery. "I can schedule the installation for Tuesday, but I want to be here personally to be sure that everything is perfect. Will you be able to make it?" This is an indirect way of formalizing the sale, and a classic use of the assumptive process. Assuming the sale is the hardest process to prepare for – but the easiest sale to make once you do.

It's not the close.
It's the open.

Can't close a sale?

It's not because you need closing skills. It's because you need selling skills. Or better stated, relationship building skills, questioning skills, and communication skills.

Every salesperson wants to know how to "close a sale." Even more want to know why they can't close some specific sale. They write me, they call me, they get frustrated, they buy books on the subject, they try, they get rejected, they get stalled, and, of course, they get lied to by their prospects.

In short, they (you) can't complete the sale.

Here's a clue. Forget closing tactics. They're worn. They're awkward. They're manipulative. And they don't put you in a very "professional" light.

Here's a bigger clue: What you have failed to uncover is the prospect's motive to buy what you're selling.

Here's the biggest clue: You're looking for a tactic when what you really need is a better strategy.

Jeffrey Gitomer

Here are 4.5 self-evaluations and idea-generators that will put your inability to close in the proper perspective.

1. **Start with questions that make the prospect consider new information:**

   - Question them about the specific value of what you sell.

   - Ask them what happened the last time they purchased what you sell.

   - Ask them how a purchase will impact their profit or productivity.

2. **Look at the way you present your product or service:**

   - Is there room for more interaction and feedback?

   - Are there times in your (boring) presentation for the prospect to talk?

   - What percent of the time does the prospect talk?

   - How compelling is your message?

   - How polished are your presentation skills?

3. **Ask questions that make the prospect look good:**
   – Ask for their opinion.

   – Ask for their feelings.

   – Ask for their expertise.

   – Ask for the benefit of their experience.

4. **Ask for the order in a way that's "assumptive" rather than "cornering."**
   Ask: "Assuming we pass this test today, Mr. Jones, when would be the perfect time to begin (deliver)?"

5. **Keep in mind that when your prospect is NOT talking, he or she is formulating impressions and opinions of you and what you sell.**
   In effect, they are deciding yes or no while you talk.

   The more you let THEM talk, the easier it will be to get those feelings and impressions revealed.

   Look at it this way. If you talk, you're selling. If they're talking, they're selling themselves.

If you still insist on a "close" try this one: "Mr. Jones, is there anything else you need to know before I enter your order?" The prospect will say "no," and you respond, GREAT!

The point of this lesson is: Not being able to close is NOT a problem. It's a symptom. The problem is: you have presented poorly, or you have created barriers, or you haven't uncovered the motives to buy, or all three.

My bet? All three.

If "not closing" is a symptom, you have to look at your selling process from the beginning, to find out where the problems or barriers are. If you do, you'll find out where the opportunities are to solidify a purchase BEFORE you get to the closing of the presentation.

It seems so logical to complete a sale *during* the presentation rather than the end. Why then, doesn't everyone do this?

One reason is that it takes more preparation, more personalized information, and more self-study before the presentation. Another is because many of the people who teach sales are still stuck in the 70s.

It seems so logical to complete a sale *during* the presentation rather than the end.

Jeffrey Gitomer

But by far, the biggest reason is that you, the supposed master salesperson, are unwilling to change your backwards pattern of: gain rapport, probe, present, overcome, and close. As long as you feel the need to close, you will be stuck there.

Maybe if you took a different view. One where you measured success from the beginning of the sales process rather than the end. Walk in. Tell the prospect that you feel he should buy from you, and that you'll make a presentation to confirm it. Then tell the prospect, "If at any time during my talk you decide NOT to buy, just ring this bell (gong) – if you don't ring, I expect at the end you'll sign the contract. Is that fair enough?"

As far-fetched as this may sound to you, I ASSURE you that it beats trying to "close" times 100. Stop thinking, "close" and establish a strategy throughout your presentation that generates a "buy."

Free Git✗Bit...Want more ideas on the close? Questions you can use to discover why customers buy? It's yours by going to www.Gitomer.com – register if you're a first-time user, and enter the words WHY THEY BUY in the GitBit box.

If your "open" isn't compelling, then your "close" will be elusive.

Jeffrey Gitomer

What are the BEST questions?

Here are a few more lead-in questions you can use at the beginning to gain rapport and understanding, and at the end to gain the order.

Tell me about the best...

Tell me about the first...

Tell me about the last time you...

Which one is your favorite...

If you could have any of these, which...

If price were no object, which would you choose...

Why do you like this one...

What would you do with it...

Where would you use it...

How would it improve...

Who would be the most impressed...

How would this help...

What makes you think...

How do you select...

What's most important to you about…

Where do you see…

How have you employed…

What has been your experience with…

If you could change one thing about…

How would you improve…

What plans have you made to…

- **Can you see any reason not to _____?**
- **Is there any additional information you need to decide?**
- **Can you see any reason not to proceed?**
- **Is there anything else (more) you need to know?**

Did you get the order? If not, here's why!

Everybody wants to close the sale. You want to close the sale, your manager wants you to close the sale. Your manager's boss wants you to close the sale. Your CEO wants you to close the sale. The accounting department wants you to close the sale. I want you to close the sale. Everybody wants you to close the sale – *except the customer.*

They don't want to be closed, and they hate salespeople that try to close. Customers want to buy. You know my mantra:

People don't like to be sold, but they love to buy.

Historically in the sales progression, the close comes at the end of the sales cycle. BUT, what you have done at the beginning of the sales cycle will most likely determine what will happen at the end of the sales cycle.

I mean, you can't say to the customer, at the end of a 6-week courtship, "I know I haven't been really good at presenting a compelling message, and I know I haven't proven my value against the competition, and I know our price is higher, so do you want to buy?" No, they're not going to buy. They're going to laugh at you. They're going to throw you out on your elliptical.

What you have done before the close will determine the outcome of the closing process.

The words "close the sale" have been around for a hundred years. I think it's time to change them. I think that if you view the close as a logical and emotional progression of the selling process, you might then understand that what has led up to the close will determine your fate. It's more of a "conclusion of part one" of the relationship building process.

Most salespeople blame the prospect when they can't close a sale. Or when the prospect won't order your product or buy your service TODAY.

It's not *their* fault, Sparky. It's *yours*. You have to start with your own outlook, and your own self-confidence. You have to visualize the sale taking place before you walk into the room, and you have to be prepared to make it once you enter.

Try this: Change your mindset. Don't *close* the sale, *assume* the sale. A good ending must be decisive, set-up, and inevitable. YOU have to be engaging, believable, passionate, and offer a compelling message. You have to be prepared with testimonials from other customers, and you have to prove that your future customer will have a positive outcome for their business. And you assume the sale is yours.

The assumptive position is the strongest selling strategy in the world.

By definition, you believe you will make every sale you attempt.

It sounds simple. It is simple – but, it's not easy. In order to utilize the assumptive close, you must be qualified.

As stated in "A few closing tactics. Taking a new look at old ways," there are two major prerequisites that make the assumptive close possible:

1. Your **personal** preparedness. People assume that everything revolves around *your product or service*, but that's not true. You have to find a balance between *product preparedness* and *mental preparedness*. You must display self-confidence, have total product knowledge, have a positive mental attitude, exude so much enthusiasm that it's contagious, and have a desire to help that exceeds a desire to earn money.

2. Your **sales** preparedness. That means that the needs of your prospect have been determined. The buying motives of the prospect are known to you. You're established as a person of value in the mind of the prospect. The prospect has confidence in you. You've removed any objections, barriers, or perceived risks they may have. And you've built solid rapport. Your job is to know everything you can about your prospect's business, their market, their needs, and their customers, their people. Know their buying motives, how they profit, and how they produce.

Now you're ready to "close" the sale. Better stated, you're ready to create the logical and emotional progression of the selling process to a happy ending.

The actual close of a sale is the delicate balance between your words and actions, and the prospect's thoughts and perceptions. And a sale is always made— either you sell them on yes, or they sell you on no. Is there one best way to close a sale? No, there are a zillion ways to close the sale. All you have to do is find the one that works best for you.

What you have done at the beginning of the sales cycle, will most likely determine what will happen at the end of the sales cycle.

Jeffrey Gitomer

Closing the sale. A mastery lesson for sales masters.

Closing the sale is a mastery of its own. It's that storybook ending that everyone's waiting for at the end of any movie or novel or children's book: "… and they all lived happily ever after."

Think about how disappointed you are when there's no clear resolution, or maybe your favorite character is killed off in the last scene – no happy ending. Same in sales, when they won't decide, when there are barriers, unspoken risk, no sense of urgency, no returned calls – there's no happy ending. Well, no happy ending for you.

Closing the sale is the *beginning of the relationship*.

At the end of the selling cycle, it's decision time. Your cards are on the table. You try to eliminate what you would call objections. You try to completely engage your prospect. You try to prove your value. And you try to show your self-confidence.

Your enthusiasm and your self-belief are closely tied to the close of the sale. How enthusiastic are you? How strongly do you believe in your company?

Closing the sale is the beginning of the relationship.

Jeffrey Gitomer

You have to believe that you work for the greatest company in the world, that your company has the greatest products and services in the world, and that you're the greatest person in the world. When you believe in yourself and your products, you're believable to your prospect.

Here are the key points to master the closing opportunity – none of which are sales techniques, ploys, or tricks:

- **People don't like to be sold, but they love to buy.** Create a buying atmosphere with questions, value, and passion.

- **Why people buy is one billion times more powerful than how to sell.** If you don't know buying motives, you'll fight price.

- **All things being equal, people want to do business with their friends.** How friendly are you?

- **If they like you, and they believe you, and they have confidence in you, and they trust you, then they MAY buy from you.** This is the NUMBER ONE RULE of sales. And the secret part of this rule is "like" is the most powerful element. If they don't like you, they'll never trust you.

- **Relationship beats price 60% of the time.**

- **Perceived value beats price 60% of the time.**

- **Remove the risks (or your prospect's perceived risks, with either you, or your company) and the sale is yours.**

- **The questions you ask determine your fate.** Great questions uncover buying motives, real needs, truth, and confidence in your understanding of the customer and his or her situation.

- **Don't make a speech.** Present a compelling message that's value driven, not product driven. Keep your conversation short and sweet. This is about them, not you.

- **Actively listen more than you talk.** Listening is not the key; *active* listening is key. Your prospect will tell you exactly what they want. But make sure you listen with *the intent to understand,* and with *the intent to respond. The two-word secret to listening isn't shut up. The two-word secret to listening is take notes.*

- **There are no "objections" in selling.** There are stalls, barriers, and risks – both real and perceived. Value, trust, proof, and buyer confidence lower barriers.

- **Challenge the prospect to do what's best for his business.** This strategy helps eliminate old relationships with other vendors that have lost value.

- **Ask for the order every time.** So simple that salespeople overlook it. Especially when the prospect poses a barrier or a stall.

Me? I assume I have the order when I walk in the door. The best close is no close. It's a combination of making a friend, presenting a compelling reason to buy, being value driven, being profit driven, being outcome driven, and assuming the sale. I hope you have enough self-confidence and self-belief to do the same.

Back to the happy ending…

One of the interesting parts about any story you've read as a child is that they all had the same sort of ending: Happy. "…And they all lived happily ever after."

NOTE WELL: In sales the key words are not "happily ever after." The key sales word is "all." "All" means the customer has to feel like they win, your company has to feel like they win, and you have to feel like you win. When everybody wins, you don't have a "deal," you don't "close the sale," you have a *relationship*. And that relationship leads to more sales.

Now that's a happy ending.

The best close is no close. It's a combination of making a friend, presenting a compelling reason to buy, being value driven, being profit driven, being outcome driven, and assuming the sale.

Jeffrey Gitomer

Closing the sale. The definitive answers you won't like.

"A – B – C. Always Be Closing."

You may know that line from the infamous sales movie *Glengarry Glen Ross* where Alec Baldwin plays a salesman. It's a throwback sales training line from the 1960s that manifested itself all the way to the 80s. The problem with that line is that some people are still using it.

Whenever I do a seminar, everyone wants to know the *fastest* way to close the sale, the *easiest* way to close the sale, and the *best* way to close the sale.

REALITY: There is no fast way, there is no easy way, and there is no best way.

However, there is a better way than thinking of it as closing the sale. And once you understand what that way is, it will change your approach to the sale, for the better, forever…

It's not the "close," it's the open.

Jeffrey Gitomer

From the moment you engage prospective customers, they're beginning to make a judgment. First they judge you, then they judge what they're buying, and finally they judge what company they're buying it from. As I've said for years, the first sale that's made is the salesperson (that would be you).

The secret of selling is four words: *perceived value* and *perceived difference*. Two of the four words are the same: *perceived*.

If your prospective customer perceives no difference between you and the competition, and perceives no value (better stated, a greater value) in what you're offering, then all that's left is price – and you will most likely lose the sale. Or if you win the sale, it will be at the expense of your profit.

There are two intangibles that, when combined, create a better chance, a better percentage, of you completing the sale. They are "comfort" and "fit." How comfortable were you with the prospective customer? How comfortable was the prospective customer with you? And was there a perceived fit? Did what you were selling fit with what the customer needed or wanted to buy?

So I'm going back to my original statement: *It's not the close, it's the open*.

Let me give you a pop quiz that will determine whether or not you were even ready to open.

How is your attitude? How strong is your belief system? Do you have a GREAT attitude? Do you have an impenetrable belief in your company, your products or services, and yourself? Do you also believe that the customer is better off having purchased from you?

How well have you researched both the company and the person that you're meeting with? Preparation for the sale is broken down into three parts: personal preparation, sales preparation, and preparation in terms of the prospect – with this critical caveat: PREPARATION IN TERMS OF THE PROSPECT.

Do you know what their reasons for buying are? Do you know what their motive(s) for buying might be? If you know their reasons and their motives, by definition, you will also know their urgency. **NOTE WELL:** Your reasons for selling pale in comparison to their reasons for buying.

When you first spoke on the phone with the prospect, was it a friendly encounter? Were you familiar with them? Were they familiar with you? Did you develop any rapport prior to arriving? Do you have anything in common?

If you know their reasons and their motives, by definition, you will also know their urgency.

Jeffrey Gitomer

Prior to your face-to-face appointment or your telephone appointment to complete the sale, and in addition to your preparation, you must have a goal for the customer to like you, believe you, have confidence in you, and trust you. If those goals are not achieved within the framework of the sales presentation, then the completion of the sale will never become a reality.

SELF-TEST: Rather than me teaching you a closing question, here are some tough questions that you must ask *yourself* before, during, and after every presentation that you make. These questions, if answered positively in the mind of the prospective customer, will preclude you from ever having to "ask a closing question."

In paraphrasing my opening statement: If it doesn't start right, it won't end right.

- **How ready were you?**
- **How friendly were you?**
- **How engaging were you?**
- **How different were you?**
- **How valuable were you?**
- **How compelling were you?**
- **How believable were you?**
- **How credible were you?**

- How self-confident were you?

- How relatable were you?

- How trustworthy were you perceived to be?

Closing the sale is not an action. It's a culmination and a sum total of the elements that make a favorable decision possible. As I've written in my *Sales Bible*, the close of a sale is a delicate balance between your words and deeds, and the prospect's thoughts and perceptions.

And a sale is always made. Either you sell the prospect on yes, or they sell you on no.

You give me a prepared, friendly, engaging, different, valuable, compelling, believable, self-confident, relatable, trustworthy salesperson – and I'll give you a sale!

Don't close the sale – rather, complete the sales process and begin the relationship.

Free Git⫪Bit...If you are interested in the eight personal barriers that you create before or during the sale, go to www.gitomer.com, register if you are a first-time visitor, and enter the word BARRIER in the GitBit box.

It's not the responsibility of the salesperson to close the sale. It's the responsibility of the salesperson to earn the sale.

Jeffrey Gitomer

Follow Jeffrey on social media and close more sales

@gitomer

/jeffreygitomer

/in/jeffreygitomer

@jeffreygitomer

/user/buygitomer

If you want the **BEST** sales training in the world, you can license Jeffrey's content.

If you're a Sales Trainer, or if you're a Sales Coach, or if you'd like to become one, you can co-brand and use Jeffrey's material and digital tools to build your own business. If you're in a corporate training department, why not license Jeffrey's material for your sales team? You can use Jeffrey's material and digital tools to make your salespeople the best on the planet.

GET THE DETAILS ➡ **GitomerCertifiedAdvisors.com**

JEFFREY GITOMER
Chief Executive Salesman

AUTHOR. Jeffrey is the author of *The New York Times* best sellers *The Sales Bible*, *The Little Red Book of Selling*, *The Little Black Book of Connections*, and *The Little Gold Book of YES! Attitude*. All of his books have been number one best sellers on Amazon. com, including *Customer Satisfaction Is Worthless*, *Customer Loyalty Is Priceless*, *The Little Red Book of Sales Answers*, *The Little Green Book of Getting Your Way*, *The Little Platinum Book of Cha-Ching*, *The Little Teal Book of Trust*, *Social BOOM!*, *The Little Book of Leadership*, and *21.5 Unbreakable Laws of Selling*. Jeffrey's books have sold millions of copies worldwide.

MORE THAN 100 PRESENTATIONS A YEAR. Jeffrey gives public and corporate seminars, runs annual sales meetings, and conducts live and virtual training programs on selling, YES! Attitude, trust, customer loyalty, and personal development. Jeffrey has also created a team of Gitomer Certified Speakers to bring his content to more audiences.

BIG CORPORATE CUSTOMERS. Jeffrey's customers include Coca-Cola, US Foodservice, Caterpillar, BMW, Verizon, MacGregor Golf, Hilton, Enterprise Rent-A-Car, AmeriPride, NCR, IBM, Comcast Cable, Time Warner, Liberty Mutual, Principal Financial, Wells

Fargo Bank, Blue Cross Blue Shield, Carlsberg, Mutual of Omaha, AC Neilsen, Northwestern Mutual, MetLife, Sports Authority, GlaxoSmithKline, *The New York Post*, and hundreds of others.

IN FRONT OF MILLIONS OF READERS EVERY WEEK.
Jeffrey's syndicated column *Sales Moves* appears in scores of business papers in the US and Europe, and is read by more than four million people every week.

ON THE INTERNET. Jeffrey's WOW website www.gitomer.com gets thousands of hits per week from readers and seminar attendees. His state-of-the-art presence on the web and e-commerce ability has set the standard among peers, and has won huge praise and acceptance from customers.

GITOMER CERTIFIED ADVISORS. Jeffrey is now licensing his classroom workshop training and online training to sales professionals around the globe. For more information, please visit GitomerCertifiedAdvisor.com.

ONLINE SALES TRAINING. GitomerVT.com is all Jeffrey, all the time. Twelve of Jeffrey's books recorded on video with interactive questions, 25 webinars, and hours of Jeffrey's real-world practical sales information, strategies, and ideas. The online

library is available 24/7/365 on your PC, tablet, and/ or smartphone – and will be continually updated as Jeffrey records new videos and content. It's ongoing sales motivation and personal inspiration.

SALES CAFFEINE. Jeffrey's weekly email magazine, *Sales Caffeine*, is a sales wake-up call delivered every Tuesday morning to more than 250,000 subscribers worldwide, free of charge. *Sales Caffeine* allows Jeffrey to communicate valuable sales information, strategies, and answers to sales professionals on a timely basis. To sign up, or for more information, visit www.salescaffeine.com.

BUSINESS SOCIAL MEDIA. Keep up with Jeffrey and his social media presence on Facebook, Twitter, LinkedIn, and YouTube. New ideas, events, and special offers are posted daily. With more than 50,000 social media followers, and more than one million YouTube views, Jeffrey has built a groundswell of attraction and engagement.

OUTSTAND. Jeffrey helped create the first CRM program that actually helps salespeople MAKE SALES, and it now has thousands of users. This incredible program must be previewed to be believed. To learn more and subscribe for a free trial, go to www .outstand.com and enter the promo code JEFFREY.

AWARD FOR PRESENTATION EXCELLENCE. In 1997, Jeffrey was awarded the designation of Certified Speaking Professional (CSP) by the National Speakers Association. The CSP award has been given fewer than 500 times in the past 25 years and is the association's highest earned award.

SPEAKER HALL OF FAME. In 2008, Jeffrey was elected by his peers to the National Speaker Association's Speaker Hall of Fame. The designation, CPAE (Counsel of Peers Award for Excellence), honors professional speakers who have reached the top echelon of performance excellence. Inductees are evaluated by their peers through a rigorous and demanding process. Each candidate must excel in several categories: material, style, experience, delivery, image, professionalism, and communication.

Index